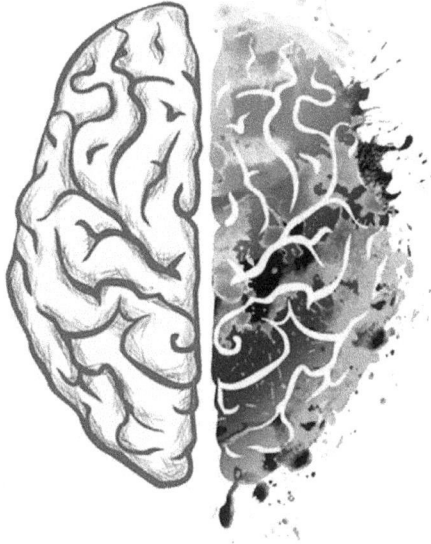

How to Lose Your Mind

52 Ways to Reprogram Your Mind
for Happiness & Success

How to Lose Your Mind:
52 Ways to Reprogram Your Mind for Happiness & Success

www.jenniferdcarroll.com

Copyright © 2017
ISBN 10: **0692830243**
ISBN-13: **978-0692830246**

Published by: uFreedom Network

How to Lose Your Mind

52 Ways to Reprogram Your Mind
for Happiness & Success

Jennifer D. Carroll

DEDICATION

This book is dedicated to my amazing mom –
Jacqueline Smith-Carroll.

You have always been an amazing beacon of
light, wisdom and inspiration my whole life.

You used quotation and story to teach me
great spiritual lessons about life and self mastery –
and now it is my privilege to pass on that
legacy of insight and inspiration.

I love you throughout all time and space.
Until we meet again. R.I.P.

CONTENTS

ACKNOWLEDGMENTS

I am grateful to my family for their love and sacrifices along the path. I am grateful for dear friends who have supported me, motivated me and believed me in the times when I didn't even believe in myself.

Special acknowledgment of love and admiration to my dad for being imperfectly perfect. I chose you so I could evolve and do what I came here to do. Thank you for being exactly what and who I needed you to be even when I didn't realize it. I love you always. (R.I.P.)

Special shouts of love to my family Uncle Edward (R.I.P.), Uncle Leonard (Lucky) (R.I.P.), Uncle Lewis (Chop), Uncle Tommy, Uncle Elliott, Aunt Sue (R.I.P.), Aunt Lynn, Aunt Pat, Aunt Dorie, Aunt Gayle, Aunt Val, Aunt Jacqueline, Uncle Richard (R.I.P.), and Aunt Daisy (Sweetie) (R.I.P.), Brother Anthony, Cousins Rhonda & Rick, Cousin Vanessa, Pam & Eric, Tamira, Sarah, Tony, and Cheston for your unwavering love and support through life's ups and downs.

Thank you to Michael Bernard Beckwith for introducing the "Life Visioning" process which taught me to surrender so I could become a channel for what is trying to express through and as me.

Special thank you to Hotep for the push and for being awesome!

I am forever grateful to the most high for all of the blessings, for keeping me safe, for always being my refuge, for always guiding me and putting the right things and right people in my life at the right time.

And to all of those not listed some of whom have loved and supported me and some of whom didn't, I honor and send love to you. Because our lives crossed paths be it for the positive or the negative – I am better.

INTRODUCTION

"You is kind. You is smart. You is important"
—Aibileen Clark,
From the Movie "The Help"

You may be rolling your eyes at the quote above,
but I don't care.

YOU NEED TO HEAR IT.

Although this movie quote is said in the cheesiest of fashions,
the sentiment holds true.

You are kind. You are smart. You are important.

That is your natural set point.

You were born that way.

Unfortunately, many of us were taught while we were growing
up that being ourselves – our TRUE SELVES – was
unacceptable. We were told that if we simply behaved
differently, spoke differently, looked differently, came from a
different place, were associated with certain people - that we
somehow would be more acceptable and receive more love
from others.

With all of these marks to our self esteem, many of us tried to fit in with our peers the best way we could, and far too often

that entailed shutting people out of the so called "in" crowd so we could feel better about ourselves.

These old school forms of bullying have now given way to online "cyber" bullying and the torment and potential psychological damage to a person's psyche can be lifelong.

I'm saying all of this to say that many of us are mentally, emotionally and spiritually damaged because we have been told in some way, shape or form - that we are not good enough.

And the crazy part about that is that **we believed them.**

But why did/do we so easily believe these things about ourselves?

Well, science has done numerous studies on human development and the science of how people learn.

According to scientific studies- when we are born, the human brain is relatively smooth and devoid of the grooves, nooks and crannies that we often see when we see an actual photo of the human brain.

As a baby develops and is exposed to its environment, it develops what I term "indentations" on the brain – the little lines that we see all throughout the brain. These indentations are basically neurological learning pathways that make a physical mark on the brain whenever something new is learned.

These indentations signal to our brain the relationship between what is being experienced and what that experience means.

For example, if the baby knows that when it cries in a certain tone it will get fed – an indentation is formed on how to get food.

If a toddler sees his parents yelling at each other and getting into a physical altercation but then an hour later they are kissing and telling each other how much they love each other, an indentation is being made into that child's mind about what constitutes love.

And the list goes on....

The whole concept is simply that the brain starts to co-relate what it sees and experiences and what that means.

So with that being said, I want you to think back for a moment and consider what indentations were programmed into your brain growing up that you are still holding on to?

Were you told that you were special, beautiful/handsome, intelligent, could do anything that you set your mind to, and were well loved; or were you told that you were stupid, couldn't do anything right, were ugly, poor and would never amount to anything?

Whichever experience you had, indentations were made on your brain that programmed you to look for things in your environment to support that belief.

Expanding on what I said earlier, I'm gonna dive a little deeper and talk about the true nature of reality.

But before I do that I want you to do something for me.

Go to this link, and watch this quick
2 minute video before you go any further:

http://www.jenniferdcarroll.com/awarenessgame

Then continue on to the next page when you are done.

So how did you do?

Did you see the guerrilla?
Did you notice the curtain changing colors?
Did you see the player with the black shirt leave the game?

If you didn't see all of those things the first time watching this video, don't worry – the vast majority of people do not notice it either.

There is in fact a specific reason why this happens and it is based on an understanding of both how the brain works as well as a quick study of quantum physics.

Scientists have discovered through the study of quantum physics that the subconscious mind absorbs roughly *6 million bits of information in its environment per second!*

So let's just say you are in a coffee shop. Your subconscious mind is analyzing information in your environment such as the temperature inside the building, the sound of your shoes on the floor as you walk in, what the woman on the opposite end of the room is doing with her fingers, the mint green color of the man's shirt that ordered the cappuccino, the slight itch you feel on your ankle because you missed that spot while putting lotion on this morning, etc.

On the opposite end, your conscious mind only takes in about *7 bits of information per second.*

Which means that there is a heck of a lot of things going on in the physical environment around you - which you are not consciously aware of.

The brain works and perceives things in its environment based on what it has been trained to look for. So the 7 things that your conscious mind sees in any given second is not based on what we would term an undisputed blanket version of "reality" but instead the version of reality that its programming and "indentations" have been trained to perceive.

Now just sit back and consider this idea.

Have you ever had a situation with someone where you felt that the person had completely acted inappropriately and was disrespectful towards you? Then after speaking to that person you realized that the person was totally oblivious to what you were upset about?

This happens because you two have different sets of indentations which are causing you to perceive the world differently.

It is not that you are right and the other person is wrong or vice versa– it is that you are both tuned in to your own individual frequency of the over 6 million bits of information.

If you introduced another 10 people of different backgrounds and upbringing, you may get 10 additional versions of "reality" that is taking place.

Do you see why it is so easy for people to fall into conflict and misunderstanding?

Most of us believe that things are unequivocally right and wrong. Black and white. However, that is not the truth.

For example, if we lived in a Hindu culture – it would be taboo to kill a cow because they are considered sacred. However, here in America, a cow is not considered sacred, a cow is considered many to just be dinner!

In some Asian cultures they eat the meat of dog, rats and insects. However here in America you can get arrested for doing any type of harm to a dog and rats and insects are considered filthy creatures unfit for consumption.

But who is right?

Whatever you consider correct or appropriate is 100% a function of what you have been programmed to believe and not some inherent truth.

Recognizing that, our perceptions and therefore our results at any given time are based on conditioning from our family, friends, society and if we are conscious enough about what is taking place – ourselves.

This book is designed to awaken you to the idea that there is indeed a multitude of possibilities taking place at any given time.

I want you to understand that YOU choose what you experience based on your awareness.

Being delayed in traffic does not have to be a bad thing – it could be something that keeps you from getting into a car accident.

Losing your job could be the best thing that has ever happened to you because now you can start a business and follow your passion.

The dissolution of a relationship could be a huge blessing because now you are free to truly be yourself without constraints.

Our judgments based on our past experiences and conditioning can be our greatest hindrances to evolution and the life we want to experience.

We can either choose to allow society and our environment to dictate what we believe and what we experience or we can get about the business of re-programming our brain so that we can see and experience what we want to see.

This book is designed to help you do just that.

In this book, I'm going to take you on a journey where I feature a powerful quote that introduces a life principle that supports success. For example, one principle that is important to develop is vision. So I will provide some perspective on what vision is, why it is necessary and how you can apply vision to get positive results in your life.

Finally, I will provide you with an affirmation which you can use to replace negative thinking and lock in a positive mindset around this particular principle, which will help you attract the outcomes you desire in life.

HOW TO USE THIS BOOK

I designed this book as a reference guide that you can use on a daily basis to reprogram your mind for success.

Why daily you may ask?

Well, you are getting conditioned on a daily basis right now and you are not even aware of it.

Between the television, the radio, the internet, magazines and other people who are under the spell – we are being told that we are not worthy, not good enough and deficient some way at every turn.

The message we are told is that if we just dressed differently, or if our hair was a certain way, or if we were smarter, or if we weren't so smart, or if we were prettier, or if we were more handsome, or if we were taller or if we were shorter or if we were lighter or if we were darker....or.... if we were more _____(fill in the blank) that somehow – we would be more worthy.

The reality is that you were born worthy. But in our capitalistic society they cannot sell you anything if you feel good about yourself. They have to convince you that something is wrong with you in some way and that their product is the "magic bullet" that can fix it.

Because we are constantly being inundated with this type of messaging, it is imperative YOU reprogram your mind – on a daily basis!

I organized the book so that you can work on one fundamental life principle for a full month.

So for example I start the book talking about the importance of "vision". My recommendation is that you take each individual quote, including the commentary and affirmation and you work with it for a full week.

Read the quote and principle first thing when you wake up in the morning, and then do the associated affirmation. You will want to recite the affirmation out loud both morning and night, preferably in the mirror and with a lot of energy and conviction.

Affirmations are an EXTREMELY important component of the reprogramming process because you are working on forming new indentations on your brain. This process helps you train your brain to sort through the 6 million bits of information that it is processing subconsciously every second of every day and identify things happening in your environment that support the reality that you want to create.

Because the affirmations are so important in this process, make sure that you read them with LOTS OF ENERGY! This is a big deal and it is very important! Your ego will usually try to take you out of this process because its job is to keep you safe which in its mind means – keeping you in the same place that you are at currently. Even if you are experiencing things that you do no want, the ego at least knows what to expect, so it will do it's best to keep you there.

If you are sincere about wanting to change your life for the better, you will want to make sure that you don't take any shortcuts and actually read the quotes, commentary and do the affirmations daily. This process is like exercising and building muscle. It takes repetition and consistency to get your results. Stay focused, be earnest in your efforts and I guarantee you will get transformational results.

Particularly when you work through each principle for a full 7 days, the daily consistency helps the principle seep into your subconscious and become part of your daily mindset.

Alternately, you can use this book as a reference guide which you pull out whenever you are going through a particular challenge and want a way to 'lose your mind' and get your thoughts back on track so you can improve your mindset and your results. Simply look up the the principle that you are struggling with and read a passage to get support in that area that you can apply to your life immediately.

I am so excited that you are on this journey and I know that if you follow the directions as outlined and stay consistent you will see a massive shift.

So let's get started!

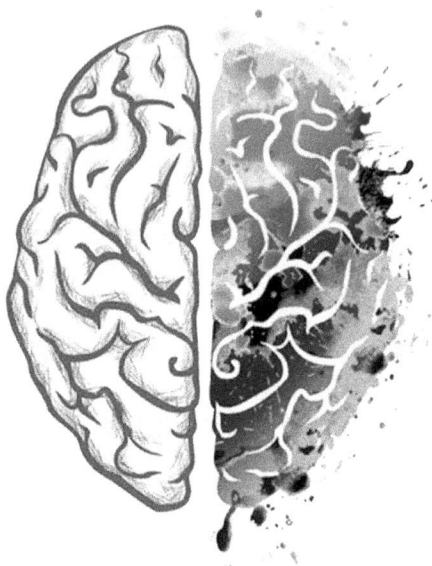

#1

VISION

Never go with the Flow – Be the Flow

-Jay Z

There are two ways that you can live in this world.

You can live the life of a visionary who forges their own path based
on where they desire to go, or you can be the reactionary
who merely responds and reacts to what other people are doing.

While the visionary creates a plan, maps out a vision and
takes steps to create that vision on a daily basis,
the reactionary person sits back and waits to see what happens.

The reactionary only takes action based on what others do;
or whatever society tells them that they can or cannot do based on
their race, gender, education, sexual orientation or religion.

**True power comes as a result of being clear on
what you really want and mapping out a plan of action
to get there.**

"I AM A VISIONARY"

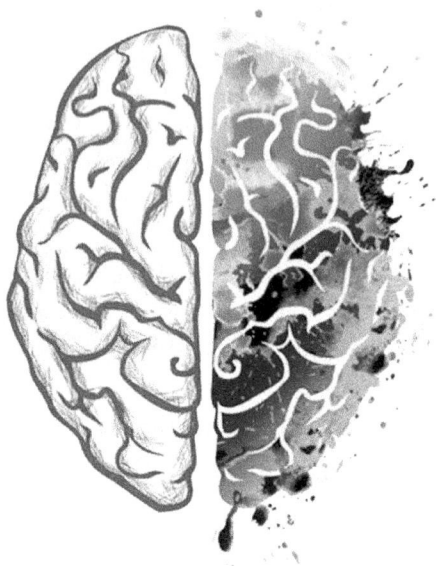

#2

VISION

You are not here merely to make a living.
You are here in order to enable the world to live more amply, with
greater vision, with a finer spirit of hope and achievement.
You are here to enrich the world, and you impoverish yourself
if you forget the errand.

-Woodrow Wilson

Our modern society has many of us so distracted
thinking about how we are going to pay the mortgage,
buy the new Mercedes and put our children in private school
that we often forget about the fact that we were born with a purpose!

A purpose that is bigger than just surviving and
barely paying the bills.

A purpose that is much bigger than buying the
latest luxury clothes and shoes.

Instead, your purpose is tied to sharing your
unique gifts with the world, in order to make a difference on the
planet and helping others on their own evolutionary journey.

**Your purpose is tied to being the change that you
want to see in the world.**

Whether it is mentoring youth
Cooking nutritious, organic meals
painting beautiful art or whatever...

What you have to offer makes a difference on the planet.

*"I AM IMPORTANT AND MY LIFE
MAKES A DIFFERENCE"*

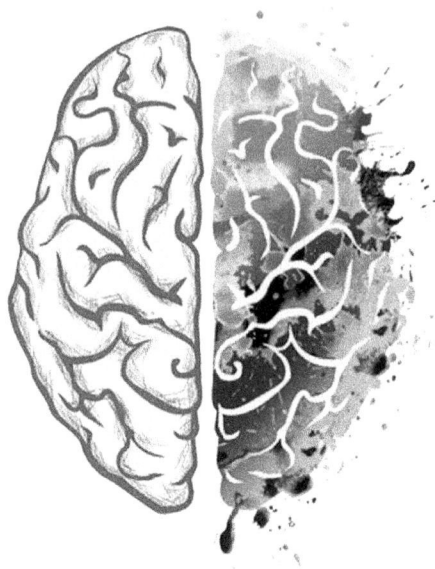

#3
VISION

It's either ownership or slave ship.
So, how are you riding?

-Hotep

Just a few decades ago the American Dream for most people was to go to college and get a degree so that they could get a well paying job, work for 30 years+ and then retire happily into the sunset with a gold watch and a turkey.

As we all know, that version of the American Dream is dead.

While the rise of technology is taking away a lot of jobs, we are also in a time in history where technology has opened up a world of opportunities for the masses of people to create financial freedom for themselves.

Indeed, the marvelous tool that we call the internet has leveled the financial playing field for those who are willing to seize the opportunity.

The question is...

Are you going to take charge of your future and create both financial and lifestyle freedom

OR

Are you going to put your financial destiny into someone else's hands?

Now is the time to develop the skills and knowledge of the new economy. If you wait, there is no doubt that you will be left behind.

"I QUICKLY AND EASILY LEARN THE SKILLS THAT ALLOW ME TO LIVE MY DREAM LIFESTYLE"

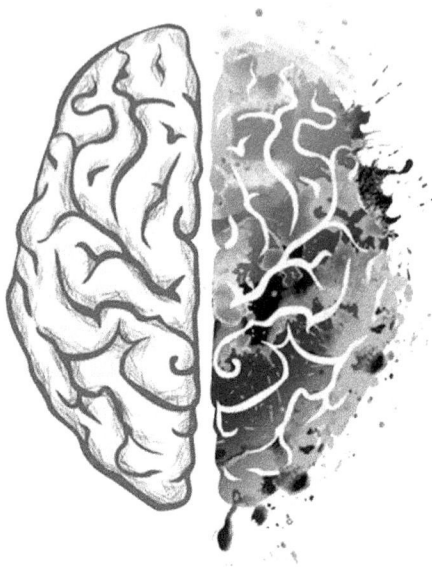

#4

VISION

Create the highest, grandest vision possible for your life,
because you become what you believe

-Oprah Winfrey

You are who YOU say that you are.

Your perception is creative and
your life is a reflection of what you believe.

What do I mean by that?

Simply stated- if you believe that the world is a
dangerous place and that people are bad and not to be trusted,
then you will find things in your environment that
will support that belief.

The people you meet will seem angry, frustrated and negative
and you will swear up and down that this is the truth.

However, the conscious mind only recognizes what it
has been trained to see and look for.

To put this even more simply:
If you are looking for something – you will find it.
However something to keep in mind is if you are NOT looking for
something – you won't find it.

There is love, abundance, peace, joy, prosperity
all around you at this very moment. However if you
are not looking for it, not expecting it, and not accepting it –
then you won't perceive it.

**Expect Things to Work Out in the Perfect Way For You and
They Will.**

"THE WHOLE UNIVERSE WORKS TOGETHER
FOR MY GOOD"

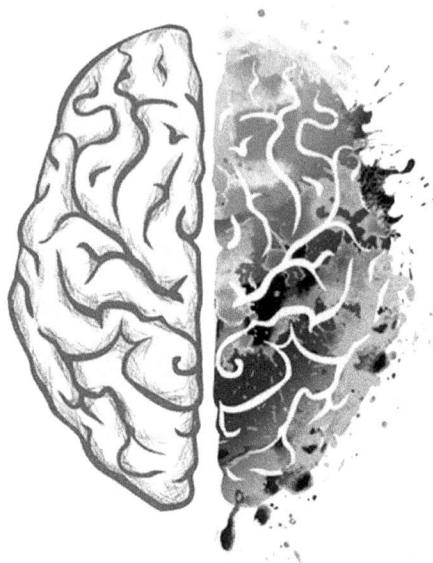

#5
LOVE

Beauty is when you can appreciate yourself.
When you love yourself, that's when you're most beautiful.

-Zoe Kravitz

Have you ever met someone who was not what society would label as traditionally attractive, but for whatever reason you found them to be amazingly beautiful?

Their eyes sparkled when they spoke.
Their smile lit up the room.
They had an inexplicable something that made them just glow from the inside.

Well, assuming that you can relate to what I'm talking about, you more than likely came into contact with someone who TRULY LOVED THEMSELF.

When you love yourself, you are not concerned with what other people say about you.

When you love yourself, you forgive yourself for your mistakes.

When you love yourself, you love your body just the same - whether you have a 6 pack or belly rolls.

When you love yourself you only allow supportive, nurturing relationships into your life.

Deliberately make time to love, forgive and reflect on the most important relationship that you will have in your lifetime -The Relationship With Yourself!

**"I LOVE AND APPROVE OF MYSELF
UNCONDITIONALLY"**

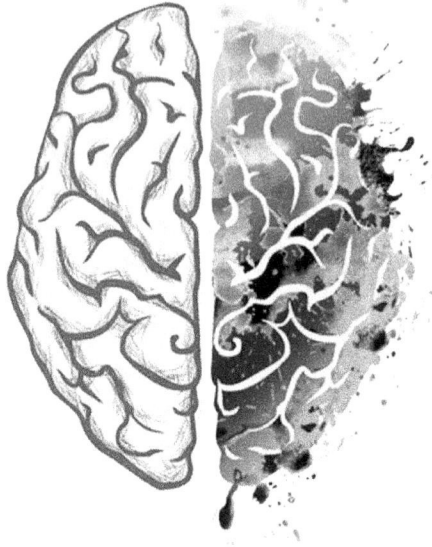

#6

LOVE

There is only one happiness in this life, to love and be loved.

-George Sand

Love is the most powerful thing in the world.

It is the invisible force that makes people want to
keep going when they feel like quitting.

It is a healing energy that can repair and renew
the body, the mind, and the spirit.

**Love is a renewable source – the more you give out,
the more is returned to you.**

Make it your mission to spread as much love as possible and
watch it come back to you abundantly in return.

"I FREELY AND HAPPILY SHARE
MY LOVE WITH OTHERS"

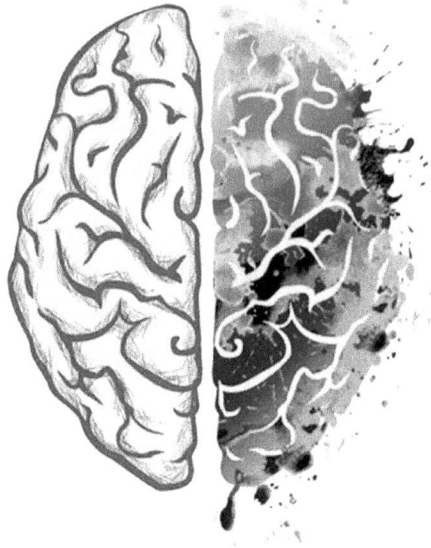

#7

LOVE

*When the power of love overcomes the love of power
the world will know peace.*

-Jimi Hendrix

Our modern day culture thrives on the idea that
Money & Power = Respect.

Popular culture positions anyone who is rich and
has a certain status, out to be someone to be admired -
regardless of what they have done to get it.

People often commit all types of atrocities on their
quest for money and power and the idea of respect that it brings.

But it's time to create a new paradigm.

One where people are respected and admired based
on the amount of love and service that they provide
to others and not how well they manipulate,
take advantage and dominate others.

LOVE >MONEY

Love is the ONLY true Power.

"I LOVE AND RESPECT PEOPLE UNCONDITIONALLY"

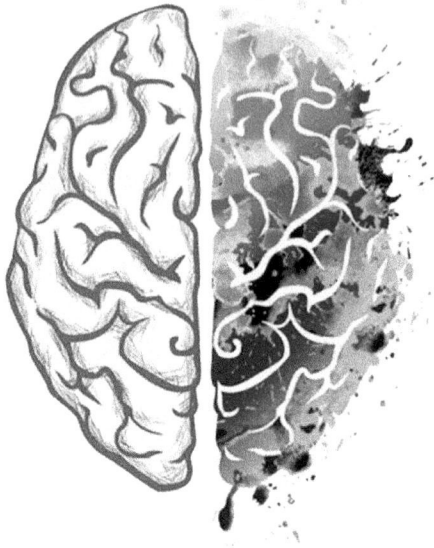

#8

LOVE

Communication is More Important Than Love

-Eric Hampton

Effective communication is one of the primary foundations of love. Without it, any relationship is built on a house of cards.

One of the biggest things that many people struggle with is being open and honest in their relationships.

People often hide their pain, loneliness and insecurity and instead of dealing with it and healing those issues, they try to project a perfect facade to those around them.

When it comes to intimate relationships, people often have a hard time being open and honest about their needs and desires for fear that the other person will reject them or not allow the space for them to be truly themselves.

So, the mask goes on - and many times people spend decades in relationships with people who do not TRULY know them.

How can you be in love with someone that you don't TRULY know? The answer is – YOU CAN'T!

The most important thing that two people can work on in a relationship is creating a space where they can not only be open and honest with each other but also reinforcing the idea that it is safe to do so. When someone feels that they are in danger of losing the other person's love as a result of being honest, that is a dangerous and alienating space to be.

True love, unconditional love – comes into play when you accept a person fully for who they truly are, without judgment and without the person making it all about them.

"I AM OPEN AND HONEST WITH THE PEOPLE THAT I LOVE, AND I ALLOW THE SPACE FOR THEM TO BE OPEN AND HONEST WITH ME"

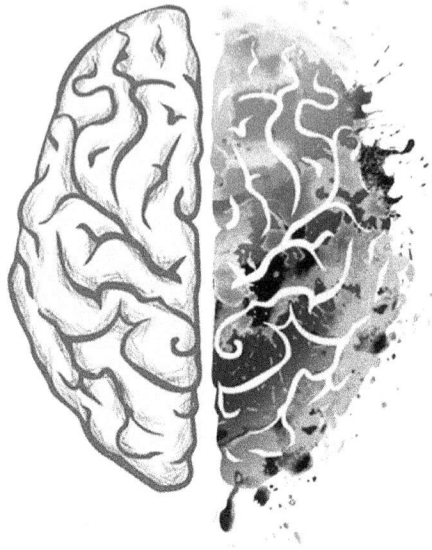

#9
PEACE

I do not want the peace which passeth understanding,
I want the understanding which bringeth peace.

-Helen Keller

There are so many times that we allow our circumstances,
other people's opinion or our own personal insecurities to keep us
restless and unfulfilled in our lives.

Often times we go through hardships and have experiences that
make us scream out "Why me!?"

Contrary to popular belief – life is not always easy
nor is it always what we would consider fair.

Life is a journey of experiences that are meant to
teach us lessons that are valuable and necessary not only
for our personal growth and evolution,
but also the growth and evolution of the planet.

We grow and evolve at a faster rate when we do not
fight the lessons that life is trying to teach us.

"I ACCEPT LIFE AND ALL OF IT'S LESSONS"

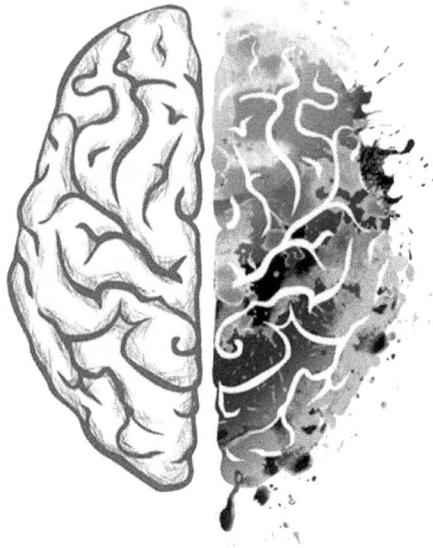

#10
PEACE

To enjoy good health, to bring true happiness to one's family,
To bring peace to all,
one must first discipline and control one's own mind.
If a man can control his mind he can find the way to Enlightenment,
and all wisdom and virtue will naturally come to him.

-Buddha

Your mind is powerful.

It is so powerful that it creates experiences based on what it has programmed to look for and associate with.

That is part of the reason why television and radio is so powerful. It exposes your brain to a message over and over and over again until your subconscious absorbs the programming.

In our life we have two choices – we can either let the world around us program our mind and our beliefs or we can consciously program ourselves with our own beliefs.

This is why it is so important to turn off the television and take control of your mind!

Some of the best ways to do this are by reading empowering books and listening to personal development audio where you can grow in your consciousness and educate yourself on subjects that can help you take your life to the next level.

Enhancing your communication skills, learning how to invest, or educating yourself on how to save more money on your taxes, it is important to always stay learning and growing.

If your life doesn't currently look the way you desire it to be, take control of what you are allowing into your mind and REPROGRAM YOURSELF with information that will take you in the direction you want to go.

"I SURROUND MYSELF WITH PEOPLE AND THINGS THAT PROMOTE LOVE, PEACE, JOY AND PROSPERITY"

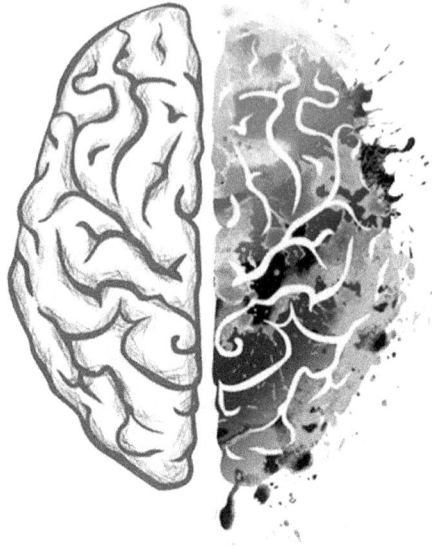

#11
PEACE

Remember one thing- through every dark night,
there's a bright day after that.
So no matter how hard it get, stick your chest out.
Keep your head up, and handle it.

-Tupac Shakur

When you are going through hardship in your life,
it feels like the trouble will last forever. It can almost seem
suffocating – like you will never come out of it.

The truth of the matter is, **trouble doesn't last always.**

As you embark on this journey called life, remember that
we can only understand light if there is darkness.

If there were no darkness we would have no concept of what the
opposite is. They both must exist for either one of them to exist,
which means that they are connected to each other.

When you are going through a hard time, remember that
everything is temporary and there is always something in
every situation that life is trying to teach you.

**The situation will last only the amount of time
that it takes for you to learn and absorb the lesson.**

Remember, there is always a rainbow at the end of a storm.

So with that in mind - look for the lesson in every hardship,
and just keep going.

**"I AM AN OVERCOMER IN LIFE
DESPITE WHATEVER ODDS I FACE"**

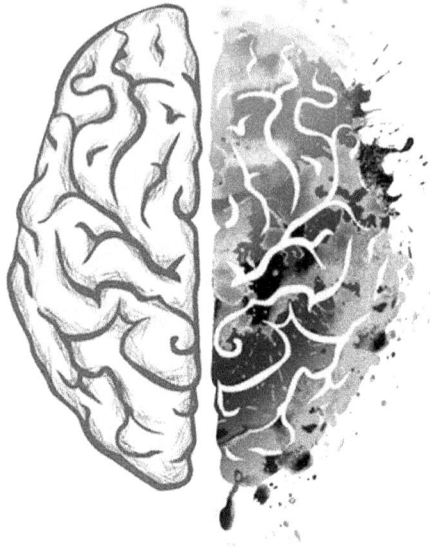

#12
PEACE

Learning lessons is a little like reaching maturity.
You're not suddenly more happy, wealthy, or powerful, but you
understand the world around you better, and you're at peace with
yourself. Learning life's lessons is not about making your life perfect,
but about seeing life as it was meant to be.

-Elisabeth Kubler-Ross

In life, you can either choose to let the things around you steal your peace of mind or you can decide to be at peace, regardless of whatever is going on in the world around you.

Peace and happiness is a decision that isn't based on the action or inaction of other people.

Your peace of mind is an inside job that only you have control over.

Remember in life that there are only two things going on at any given point in time -

You are either winning or you are learning a lesson that will give you the tools to win.

So in essence, you stay winning!

"ALL I DO IS WIN, NO MATTER WHAT"

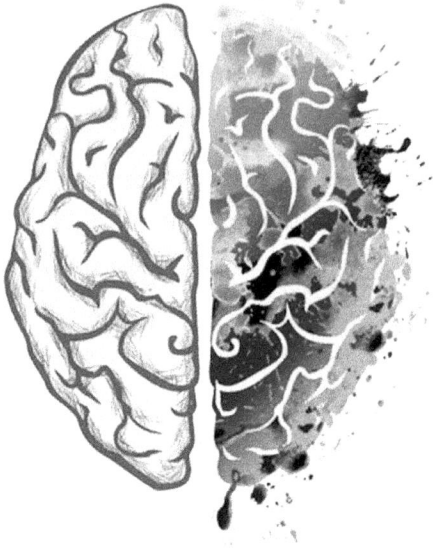

#13
HAPPINESS

There may be Peace without Joy, and Joy without Peace, but the two combined make Happiness.

-John Buchan

Seek out joy.
Seek out peace.
Create happiness.

Sometimes we can allow ourselves to be placed into situations that steal our joy and our peace and we become stressed out, out of balance, or depressed.

It is MANDATORY that we seek relationships, and environments that bring us a sense of peace and joy.

When you lack peace and joy in your life, you are unable to make clear decisions because you are operating on empty spiritually.

Staying on empty spiritually and emotionally can keep you on a perpetual cycle of mediocrity.

Remember, when you make the decision to be happy – you will be.

"I AM PEACEFUL, I AM JOYFUL, I AM HAPPY"

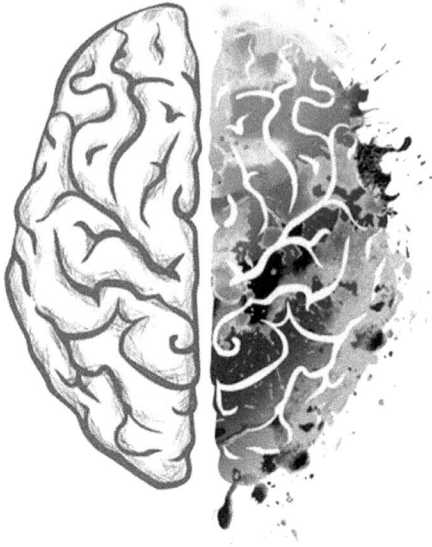

#14

HAPPINESS

Success is not the key to happiness. Happiness is the key to success.
If you love what you are doing, you will be successful.

-Albert Schweitzer

It's amazing how many people believe that if they are
"successful" by society's standards, they will suddenly be happy.

Every day people make decisions not based on what
they want to do or what brings them joy, but merely
because societal and social pressure is making they feel
that is "what they are supposed to, should do, or should want".

They trap themselves in dead end jobs, succumb to empty
unfulfilled careers and bad relationships – simply because
they have been told by someone else
"This is what success looks like".

The truth of the matter is, success looks different for everyone.

The thing that might make you feel happy and successful -
might make the next person feel like an unproductive, loser.

Only YOU can define what true success & happiness is to you.

Just rest assured, if you spend your time doing exactly
what you love, your passion and excitement will fuel
your success and cause you to prosper ABUNDANTLY!

**"I AM DOING WHAT I LOVE AND GETTING PAID
HANDSOMELY FOR IT"**

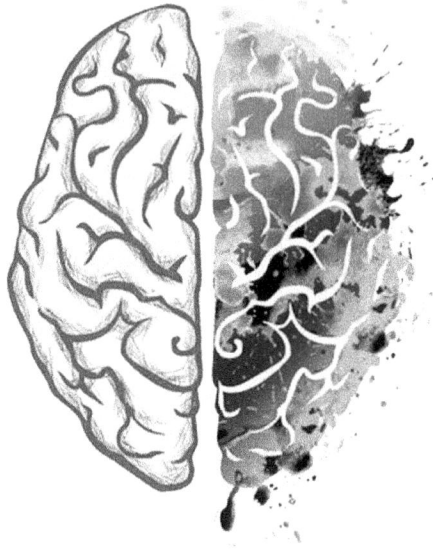

#15
HAPPINESS

Let us never know what old age is.
Let us know the happiness time brings, not count the years.

-Ausonius

Age is just a number.

It means nothing other than the meaning that is placed on it.

For many, growing older is a depressing experience
fueled by the idea that somehow their best years are behind them.

The truth is – being older in age simply means that you have been
around long enough to have a ton of experiences, learn a variety of
lessons and celebrate plenty of wins.

As you get older you will find happiness if you know that you
have lived fully and blessed the planet with your unique gifts.

Celebrate your age...you are just getting BETTER!

**"AS I GET OLDER, I GET WISER
AND BETTER IN EVERY WAY"**

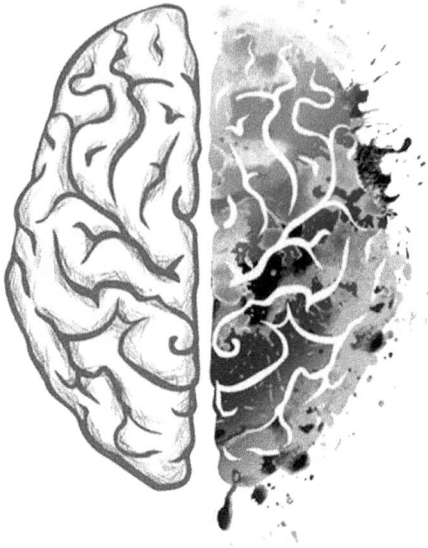

#16
HAPPINESS

Every day is a new day, and you'll never be able to find happiness if you don't move on.

-Carrie Underwood

Life can be hard and sometimes very painful.

As you go along life's journey the unexpected will happen and challenges will come. Always remember that tomorrow is a new day, full of new opportunity.

Choose to let go of the challenges of yesterday, so that you don't keep reliving something that already happened.

In your release you will have the ability to find true happiness TODAY!

"I SURRENDER TO NEW OPPORTUNITIES TO PROSPER EVERY DAY"

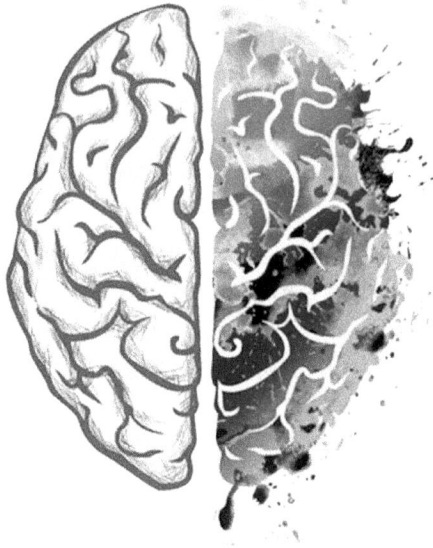

#17
FRIENDSHIP

Friends, How many of us have them?
Friends, Ones we can depend on
Friends, How many of us have them?
Friends. Before we go any further, let's be...

Friends is a word we use everyday
But Most the time we use it in the wrong way
Now you can look the word up again and again
But the dictionary doesn't know the meaning of friends.

-Whodini

What does the word – FRIENDS – mean to you?

If you ask 10 people, you could easily come up with
10 different answers.

**When entering into a relationship with someone,
it is important to find out if they share your same
opinion and definition about what friendship is.**

Often times we make assumptions that people have the
same philosophy on relationships that we do, and when
they don't live up to these internal expectations,
we are hurt and upset.

The reality is, everyone has different perspectives based
on their background and experiences.

Model what it means by your own actions and clearly
communicate your desires with those you are in relationship
with so there is no room for confusion.

**"I ALWAYS TREAT PEOPLE
HOW I WANT TO BE TREATED"**

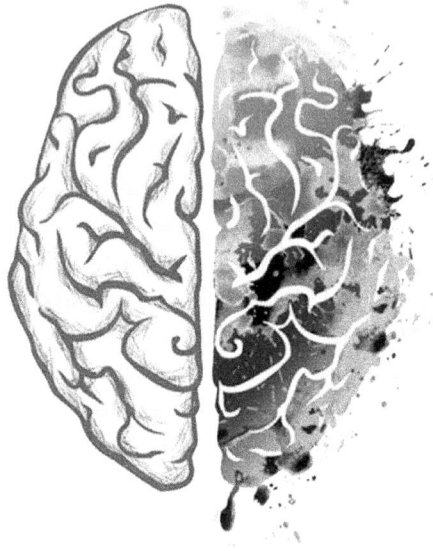

#18
FRIENDSHIP

The truth is, everyone is going to hurt you.
You just got to find the ones worth suffering for.

-Bob Marley

Some people believe the statement that says
"people that care about you, never hurt you."
However, that statement is not true.

They may not set out to hurt you- but often time's people
unintentionally do things that hurt us deeply.

What we must realize is that what they are doing is not
necessarily being done in malice, but is likely just an unconscious
response to pain and anger from past experiences.

Experiences which they may have never dealt with.

Long story short – everything is not about you.

It may affect you, but it's not ABOUT YOU.

Take time to ponder the underlying cause of why that
person is doing what they are doing.

If you don't think they are worth the trouble – dismiss them from
your life, but if you care and want them in your life - take the time
to exercise compassion and understanding towards them.

**"I LOVE AND ACCEPT MY FRIENDS
AND FAMILY UNCONDITIONALLY AND
I CHOOSE NOT TO TAKE THINGS PERSONALLY"**

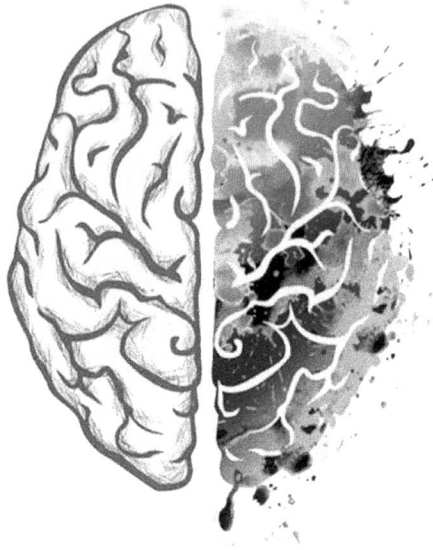

#19

FRIENDSHIP

Sometimes being a friend means mastering the art of timing. There is a time for silence. A time to let go and allow people to hurl themselves into their own destiny. And a time to prepare to pick up the pieces when it's all over.

-Octavia Butler

One of the biggest mistakes that we can make in our relationships is to try to save people from the lesson that life is trying to teach them.

It's natural to want to help people and attempt to save people that you care about from having to go through certain hardships.

However, often times what happens is you do nothing but ostracize the relationship because they are not ready or don't want to hear your advice.

It's during those times that we just need to learn how to step back and let that person go through whatever experience that they need to go through and learn the lesson that they need for their soul's evolution.

When you stand in the way, you stop the growth.

"I TRUST THE PROCESS OF LIFE AND UNDERSTAND THAT EVERYTHING WORKS TOGETHER FOR GOOD."

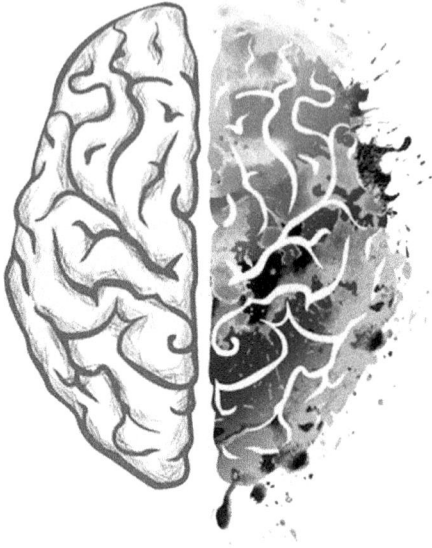

#20
FRIENDSHIP

You can make more friends in two months by becoming interested in other people, than you can in two years by trying to get other people interested in you.

— Dale Carnegie

People LOVE people that are interested in them.

People who share their interests, think that they are smart, resourceful, good looking, etc.

Those types of people always get other people's attention.

If you want to develop and nurture more friendships, deeper friendships and better friendships, learn to look for the good in other people.

"I CONSTANTLY LOOK FOR THE GOOD IN OTHER PEOPLE"

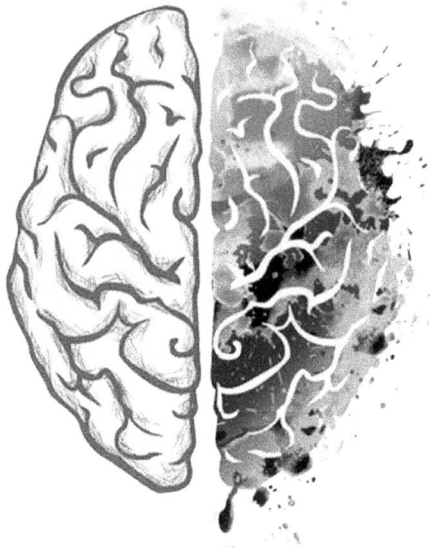

#21
FORGIVENESS

When you haven't forgiven someone who has hurt you,
You turn your back against your future.
When you do forgive — you start walking forward.

-Tyler Perry

Forgiveness can be one of the hardest things for someone to do, but it is in fact one of the most necessary endeavors that we can undertake.

When you live in a space where you will not forgive someone who you feel has wronged you, you are basically just keeping your eyes focused on the past and reliving the situation – over and over and over again.

You cannot move forward into a new and bright future – if you are looking behind you with an energy of pain, hate and resentment.

Focusing too much on your past will stall the good that is trying to flow into your life right now.

Release, let go and FORGIVE!

"I CHOOSE TO FORGIVE OTHERS SO I CAN MOVE FORWARD INTO MY DESTINY"

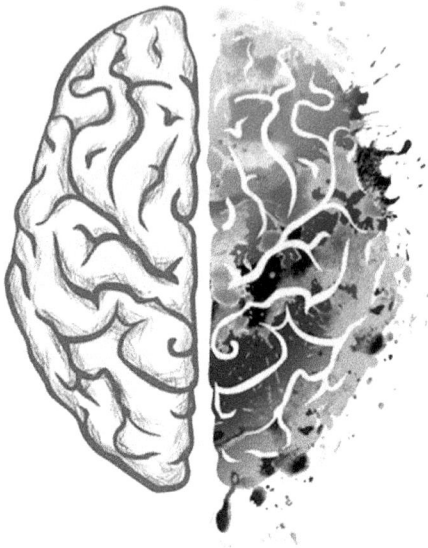

#22

FORGIVENESS

Inner peace can be reached only when we practice forgiveness.
Forgiveness is letting go of the past, and is therefore the means
For correcting our misconceptions.

-Gerald Jampolsky

There is a saying that goes
'we see the world not as it is, but how WE are'.

If we hold a certain belief system or world view – then we will
continue to perceive and experience things which
support that world view.

For example – have you ever met a woman who says things like
"All men are dogs." or "All men are liars"?

Then when you examine further you find that she is ALWAYS
attracting men who behave like dogs and liars to her?

Lack of forgiveness clouds our perception in a major way, because
when we hold a particular belief system, we tend to push away or
ignore things that do not support our belief system.

Using the woman in this example, she is likely ignoring men that do
not act like dogs and who do not lie to her because she has been
trained to look for the doggish, lying type of man.

In order for the healing to take place, this person must practice
forgiveness of those that hurt her so she can not only release the
pain, but also release her attachment to that experience so she can
stop projecting it on to other people.

**If you want to attract positive, loving people into your life -
learn to expect positive, loving people to appear.**

The first step on this journey is forgiveness.

"I HAVE INNER PEACE BECAUSE I LOOK FOR THE BEST IN OTHER PEOPLE!"

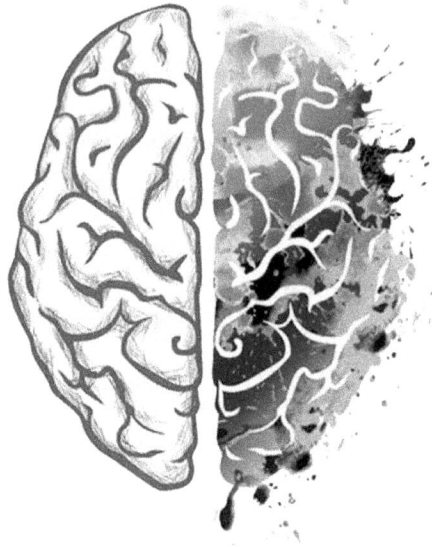

#23

FORGIVENESS

For me, forgiveness and compassion are always linked.

*How do we hold people accountable for wrongdoing
and yet at the same time*

*Remain in touch with their humanity enough to believe in their
capacity to be transformed?*

-bell hooks

Hurt people, hurt people...
and there are a TON of hurt people in the world.

Most people don't take the time necessary to examine
the life issues that have caused them pain and scarred
their spirit and instead they merely just"keep it moving".

The problem with this is that these same people then
turn around and likely perpetuate the same hurtful things
which were done to them, onto others.

Have you noticed how many people who grow up with
alcoholic parents, become alcoholics?

Or people who were molested as children may turn
around and do the same thing to a child?

Is it really that this person is a complete monster?

Or is it that this is a person who has been scarred and has never
taken or been given the opportunity to heal?

Learn to practice compassion when interacting with others,
because it is likely that they are victims of someone else's
dysfunction – just like you.

**"I FORGIVE OTHERS IN THE SAME MANNER
THAT I WANT TO BE FORGIVEN"**

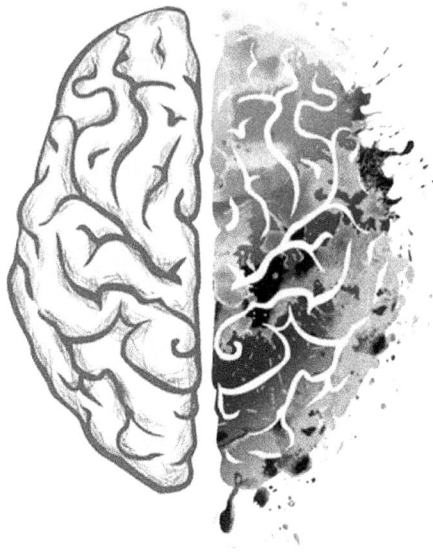

#24
FORGIVENESS

Be kind, for everyone you meet is fighting a hard battle.

-Philo

Have you ever seen someone battle it out and go crazy
over a parking space or in traffic?

You may have seen them screaming at the top of their lungs,
veins bulging, banging on the steering wheel, freaking out...
and then just wondered to yourself what the heck is this person's
deal?

Sometimes we can get so upset and angry at the actions of
others and not realize that what we are experiencing, may
not be what is really going on.

That person may be going through an ugly and painful divorce.
Their teenager may have just run away from home.
They may have just lost their parent to a painful bout with cancer.

There are a thousand scenarios of what is truly going on with that
person. But of course you don't know this – you just see CRAZY!

**Consider the idea when someone pisses you off or
rubs you the wrong way, they may be dealing with something
that you don't understand and have no idea about.**

Extend to them benefit of the doubt.
Every person is battling something.

**"I BELIEVE PEOPLE ARE GOOD AND I GIVE
EVERYONE THE BENEFIT OF THE DOUBT"**

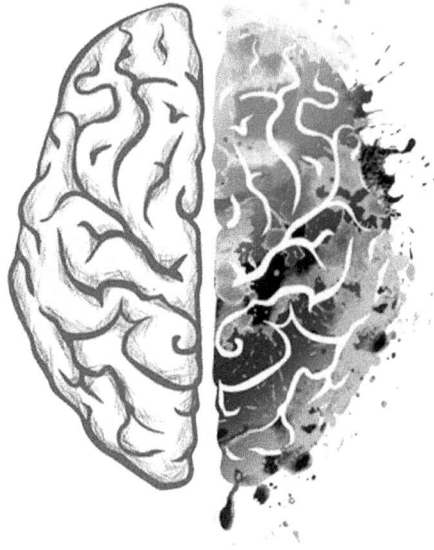

#25
HOPE

Hope is not blind optimism.
It's not ignoring the enormity of the task ahead or
the roadblocks that stand in our path.
It's not sitting on the sidelines or shirking from a fight.
Hope is that thing inside us that insists, despite all evidence to the contrary,
that something better awaits us if we have the courage to reach for it,
and to work for it, and to fight for it.

Hope is the belief that destiny will not be written for us, but by us,
by the men and women who are not content to settle for the world as it is, who
have the courage to remake the world as it should be.

-Barack Obama

The world can be an unfriendly place – one that many
experience as a place of pain, trauma, hopelessness and despair.

Poverty, abuse, lack of opportunities, and discrimination
can close in on a person's psyche causing them to believe
that their life has no value and that they in turn have nothing to lose.

This is one of the most dangerous states that an individual and a
society can be in.

When you have people who have given up to the point
that they do not care if they live or die, when they lose hope that
things will be better tomorrow – you have the makings for
a very dangerous society.

**On the other hand, hope is one of the most
powerful forces in the world.**

It is a guiding light that shines on the unknown
and makes the seemingly impossible, possible.

When a person has hope, they get that dose of inspiration and a
vision for a brighter tomorrow, which can be the simple
push that they need to keep on going.

"I AM CONSTANTLY FOCUSED ON A VISION FOR A BRIGHTER TOMORROW"

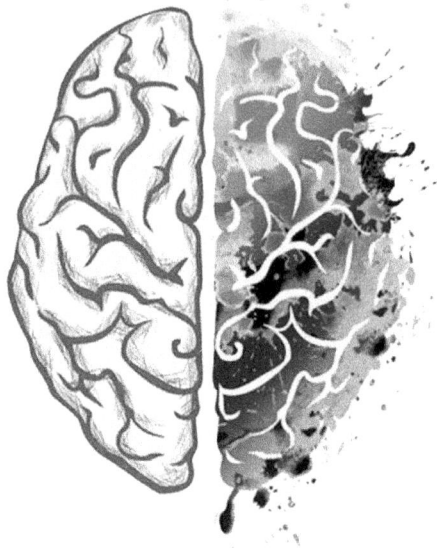

#26
HOPE

Each time a man stands up for an ideal,
or acts to improve the lot of others,
or strikes out against injustice,
he sends forth a tiny ripple of hope,
and crossing each other from a million different centers of energy
and daring, those ripples build a current that can sweep down
the mightiest walls of oppression and resistance.

-Robert Kennedy

We are all in this thing called life together.

Many people are indifferent to the struggles of those around them,
under the false notion that the injustice which others
experience does not affect them.

However nothing could be further from the truth.

As Dr. Martin Luther King, Jr. once said –
'A Threat to Justice Anywhere is a Threat to Justice Everywhere'.

The things that affect our neighbor are the same things
that have a way of eventually affecting us.

We are indeed our brother's keeper.

In order to live in a functional and healthy society, we all
should take an interest in making sure that justice
is handed down fairly.

"I AM MY BROTHERS KEEPER"

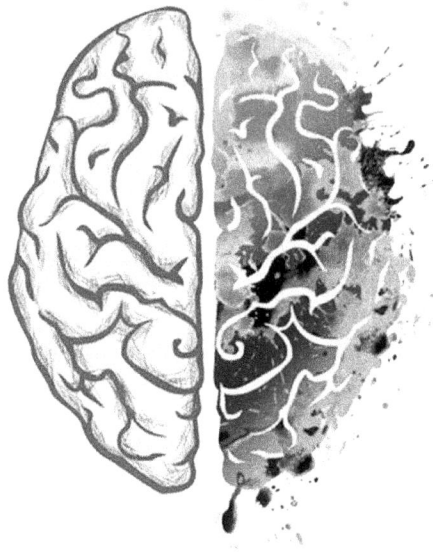

#27
HOPE

We talk a lot about hope, helping, and teamwork.
Our whole message is that we are more powerful together.

-Victoria Osteen

There is power in a group of people coming together
for a common good.

**The thread that holds an alliance of like minds together
is the simple idea that the whole is stronger
than the individual parts.**

If you are serious about seeing a positive change in the world,
you must come out of isolation and align with others who have
similar interests and desire to make an impact for the common good.

There is power in good people coming together to take action and
be the change that they want to see.

"I ATTRACT PEOPLE INTO MY LIFE WHO HELP SUPPORT MY MISSION"

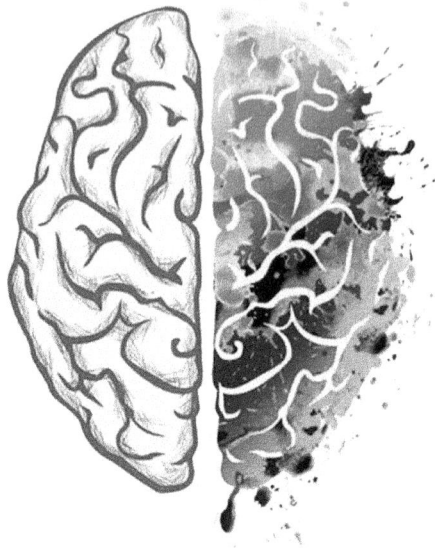

#28
HOPE

Miracles happen every day.
Change Your Perception of What a Miracle is and
You Will See Them All around You.

-Jon Bon Jovi

The fact that you woke up this morning is a miracle.

The fact that you are breathing air without having to consciously think about it - is a miracle.

The fact that you have seen all you have seen and
been through all that you've been through is a miracle!

Miracles happen everyday.

Adjust your perception and dwell in the frequency of gratitude for everything that you have been blessed with - seen and unseen!

"I LIVE A MIRACULOUS LIFE DAILY"

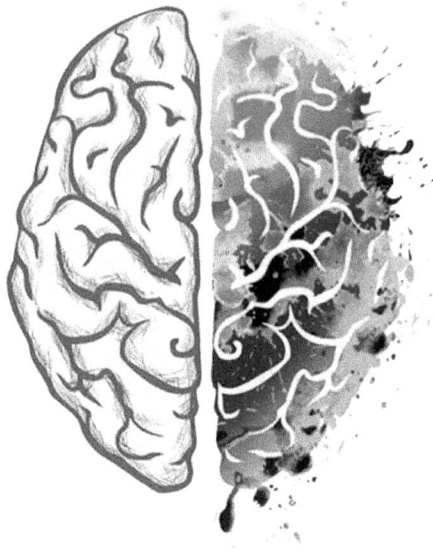

#29

ABUNDANCE

Abundance is not something we acquire.
It is something we tune into.

-Wayne Dyer

There are over 6 million possibilities of things taking place
every second of every day which our minds can focus on.

What we perceive from all of the available stimuli that our mind
comes into contact with is based on whatever we are tuned into
at any given moment.

**If you are experiencing lack, depression or loneliness,
it is because you are focused on what you don't have,
wishing something in your life was different than the way it is
and wishing that you had someone to distract you from
everything that you feel isn't working in your life.**

However if you tune yourself into the abundance
that is all around you - you will begin to see more clearly
all of the people in your life that help, love and support you.

If you tune yourself into the abundance that is all around you -
you will start to perceive the simple blessings that we often
take for granted – like having food to eat every day,
a roof over your head and clean water to drink.

There is so much abundance around us all of the time,
but many of us don't see it because we are too focused on
what we THINK we don't have.

Learn to tune your attention towards abundance and watch as it
multiplies in your daily life.

"MY LIFE IS ABUNDANT IN EVERY GOOD WAY"

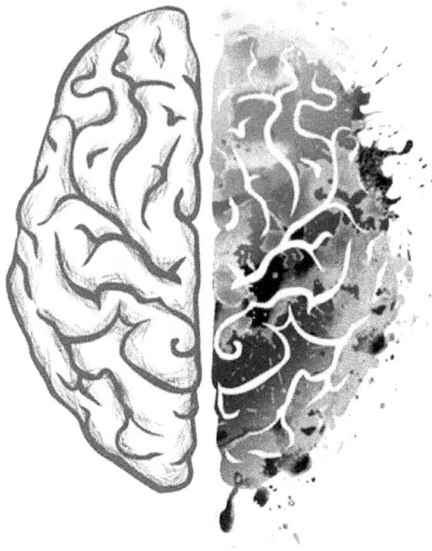

#30

ABUNDANCE

*The universe operates through dynamic exchange...
giving and receiving are different aspects of the
flow of energy in the universe.*

*And in our willingness to give that which we seek,
we keep the abundance of the universe circulating in our lives.*

-Deepak Chopra

We have all likely heard the statement "you reap what you sow". This statement simply means that if you plant something - let's just say a corn seed for example, you would not then turn around and harvest tomatoes.

Life works the same way.

If we want to reap love, joy, peace, abundance, and prosperity – then we have to sow those same principles into the lives of others.

If you are sowing anger, resentment, unforgiveness and animosity you will reap accordingly.

Be mindful of what you sow!

"I LIVE, BREATHE AND BREATHE AND HAVE MY BEING IN A STATE OF CONSTANT ABUNDANCE AND OVERFLOW"

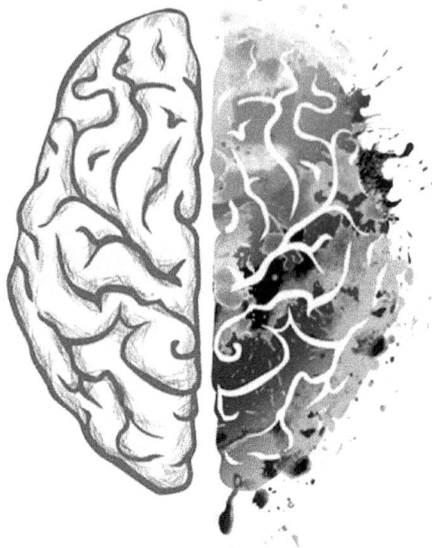

#31
ABUNDANCE

People with a scarcity mentality tend to see everything in terms of win-lose. There is only so much; and if someone else has it, that means there will be less for me. The more principle-centered we become, the more we develop an abundance mentality, the more we are genuinely happy for the successes, well-being, achievements, recognition, and good fortune of other people. We believe their success adds to...rather than detracts from... our lives.

-Stephen R. Covey

We live in a world of unlimited abundance.

However - some people believe that if someone else prospers abundantly, somehow they will have less as a result.

Often times when people come across individuals that are living in high levels of abundance, they say things such as
"That person doesn't need all of that" or "they must have taken advantage of people in order to get that much money"

When we talk like that, we are pushing our own abundance away from us, because we are telling our subconscious "I don't need all that" or "In order to get rich I will have to take advantage of people."

Many people hold the subconscious belief that rich people are bad, but then on a conscious level they desire to be rich.

The principle of abundance doesn't work like that.

You must remember that the subconscious mind is substantially more powerful than the conscious mind, and it ALWAYS WINS.

Therefore if you believe subconsciously that rich people are bad, the subconscious mind usually also does not want to be bad –
so it will put you in positions that sabotage your ability to achieve abundance at higher levels.

If you truly want unlimited abundance to flow into your life – learn to be happy for the prosperity of others.

"I HONOR AND CELEBRATE MY ABUNDANCE BY CELEBRATING THE ABUNDANCE OF OTHERS."

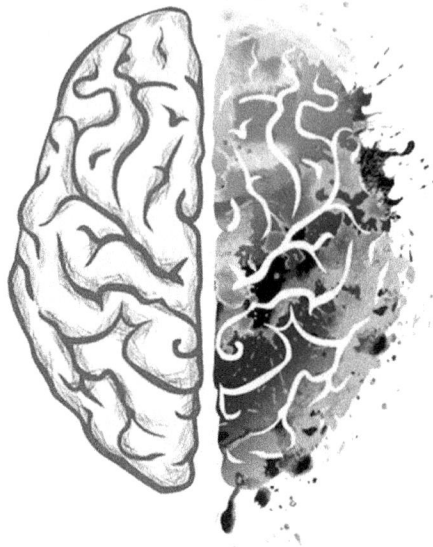

#32

ABUNDANCE

The fastest way to bring more wonderful examples of abundance into your personal experience is to take constant notice of the wonderful things that are already there.

-Esther Hicks

We see the world not as it is, but instead based on how we are.

If you are in a place where you are not experiencing the love, joy and abundance that you would like to experience - then you need to spend more time dwelling in GRATITUDE!

Gratitude is a blessing multiplier.

The more you express gratitude for all that you have, all that you are and for the protection that has kept you safe in ways both seen and unseen – the more you will witness more and more blessings flowing into your life.

One of the most effective ways to practice gratitude on a daily basis is to write down at least 3 things that you are grateful for every day before you go to bed.

If you engage in this practice every day, you will realize the abundance of things that you have to be grateful for!

"EVERY DAY IN EVERY WAY, I AM GRATEFUL FOR ALL THAT I HAVE."

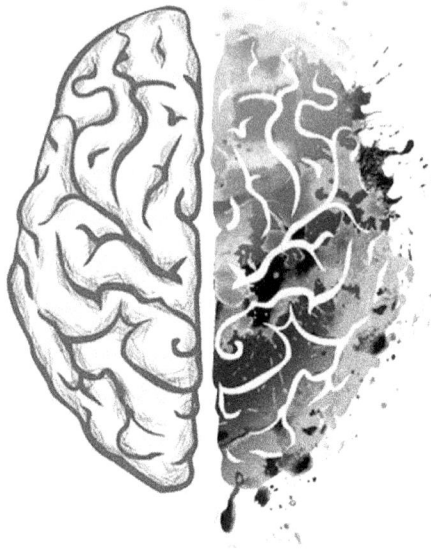

#33

SELF ESTEEM

It seems we living the American Dream,
But the people highest up got the lowest self-esteem.
The prettiest people do the ugliest things
for the road to riches and diamond rings.

- Kanye West

One of the biggest lessons that I have had to learn along my own life journey was to rely on self referral instead of object referral.

What does that mean you ask?

Well, object referral is when a person identifies themselves and their self esteem based on things outside of themselves - such as what kind of car they drive, what kind of house that they live in and what they do for a living.

So basically they will only feel good, feel validated and feel worthy if the objects – (the car, the house, the job title, etc) are there.

So if life changes and they get downsized from their job, they lose their life savings because of a dive in the economy, or they just no longer have the "stuff" on which they have come to rely, these same people are ready to self medicate or jump off a building because they no longer know who they are!

On the other hand, a person who uses self referral realizes that they are worthy just because they are a child of God.

They understand that their value is not dependent on things outside of themselves because all of those things are temporary and can change. When a person practices self referral they have true power because they understand that THEY control their environment and what happens to them and not the other way around.

When you know who you are internally, you have nothing to hide and nothing to prove. That realization is your REAL point of power.

"I AM WORTHY NOT BECAUSE OF ANYTHING I HAVE BUT SIMPLY BECAUSE I AM ME"

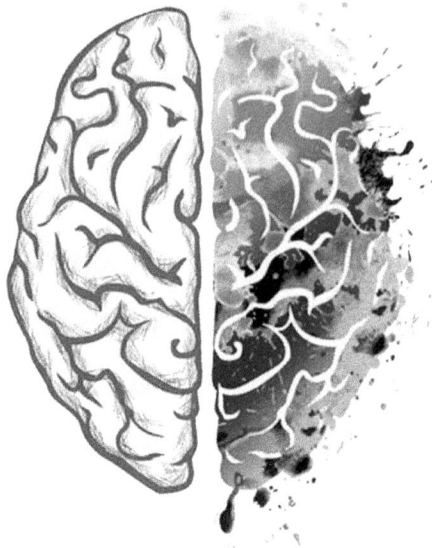

#34
SELF ESTEEM

*To be nobody but yourself in a world which is doing its
best, night and day, to make you everybody else -
means to fight the hardest battle
which any human being can fight; and never stop fighting.*

-e. e. Cummings

Have you ever noticed that you can't turn on the T.V., listen to the radio, and open up a magazine or even just log on to the internet without being hit with some type of advertisement?

We are all constantly being told in one way or another that we are too fat, too skinny, too tall, too short, not smart enough, too smart, too dark, too light, not healthy enough, too healthy, too young, too old…

Basically whatever you are, advertisers and the media wants you to believe that the opposite is better, so they can sell you something!

The truth is and will always be that you are PERFECT JUST THE WAY YOU ARE.

There is nothing to add, there is nothing to subtract.

Contrary to what they would have you believe... the latest pill, cream, lotion or potion won't make it so.

In all of your perfect, "imperfections"- YOU ARE ENOUGH.

"I AM ENOUGH!"

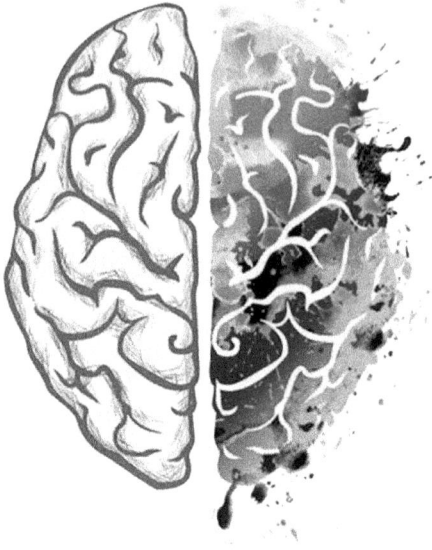

#35

SELF ESTEEM

Until you value yourself, you won't value your time.
Until you value your time, you will not do anything with it.

—M. Scott Peck

A lot of people don't value themselves.
I used to be one of them.

At one point in my life I would constantly give my time freely to individuals and situations that did not offer me back anything in return.

As I have gotten older I recognize that time is indeed our most precious asset which means that I am serious about leveraging my time in ways that will allow me to grow and reach the goals that I have set for myself.

If you are constantly spending your time watching TV, hanging out at the club, playing video games or just generally spending your time on things that are not going to take you from where you are – to where you want to be; you may want to take a hard long look in the mirror to figure out if you REALLY believe that you deserve what you say that you want in life.

Life is short, so it's a good idea to make sure that you make the time that you have count.

Take the time to live like no one else now, so that later you can live like no one else.

"I HONOR MYSELF BY HONORING MY TIME"

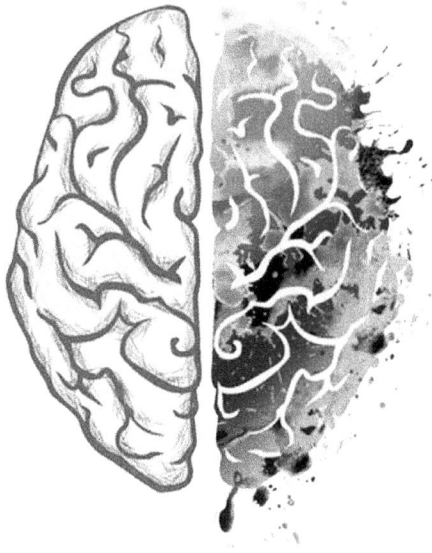

#36

SELF ESTEEM

Love yourself first and everything else falls into line.
You really have to love yourself to get anything done in this world.

–Lucille Ball

Have you ever went shopping and bought yourself a new outfit, and literally felt like a million bucks?

You couldn't wait to wear that new outfit because you knew how good it looked on you. When you put it on, it seemed that people responded to you differently, that the opposite sex was more friendly and receptive to you and your overall swag had jumped up to 100 trillion!

Well the truth of the matter is - it wasn't really the clothes. It was how you FELT in the clothes.

YOUR CONFIDENCE.

And because you felt more confident, things began to magically just fall in place in a magnificent way. Confidence and self esteem is a magical energy that attracts what you want to you.

When people feel that you believe that you are freaking awesome...

They start to treat you like you are freaking awesome!

It all begins and ends with you!

"PEOPLE TREAT ME THE WAY
THAT I TREAT MYSELF"

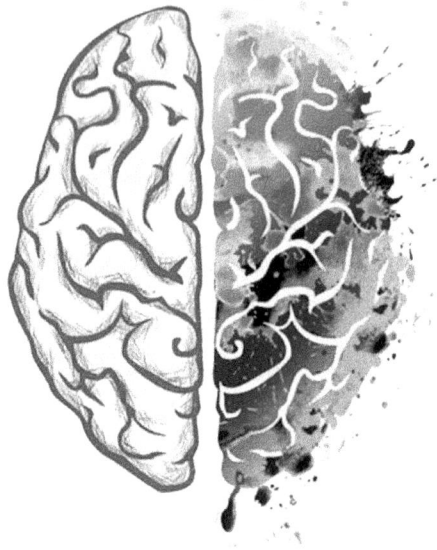

#37

DISCIPLINE

We must all suffer one of two things: the pain of discipline or the pain of regret or disappointment.

-Jim Rohn

Growth is never easy.

It can be uncomfortable and inconvenient. But very necessary.

If you want to experience or have something that you have never had, you are going to have to do something that you have never done likely in a way that you may have never done it.

That generally means that you are going to have to learn new skills, break up your routine, and do some things that you don't necessarily want to do.

Discipline is the process of giving up what you want right now for the thing that want more.

"I GET WHAT I WANT BECAUSE I AM WILLING TO DELAY GRATIFICATION."

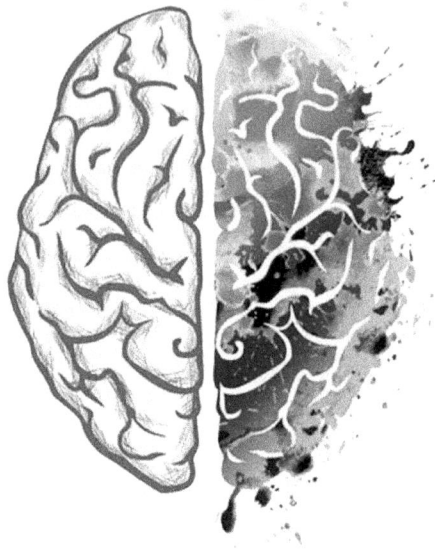

#38

DISCIPLINE

Talent without discipline is like an octopus on roller skates. There's plenty of movement, but you never know if it's going to be forward, backwards, or sideways.

-H. Jackson Brown, Jr.

Many years ago I worked in the music industry and during that time I befriended a girl who was a super talented musician. She was not only an amazing song writer, and vocalist – she also played 4 musical instruments.

She was incredibly talented!

At one point she was signed to a major record label and had gone into the studio to record the album that she had visualized doing for many years.

But unfortunately it never was completed nor did it ever come out.

Why you ask?

Well, she got full of her own hype and didn't take the opportunity that she had in front of her seriously.

She missed studio sessions.
Showed up high and drunk.
Long story short...her record label dropped her.

By then, she had developed a reputation as being difficult and unreliable and so she had trouble getting re-signed...
and her career never recovered.

Her talent couldn't save her. Her contacts couldn't help her.

At the time, she lacked the discipline that was needed to successfully complete her project, but by the time she figured it out and made steps to correct it, it was too late.

Moral of the story:
Don't take your talent and natural abilities for granted – practice discipline to turn your dreams into reality.

"I AM DISCIPLINED AND FOCUSED ON MY GOALS"

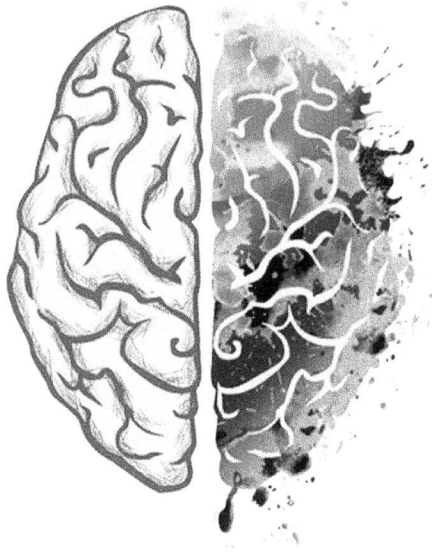

#39

DISCIPLINE

If we do not discipline ourselves the world will do it for us.

-William Feather

Many people think that they can ignore their health with
no problem.

They drink, smoke, don't get adequate sleep, are under stress,
have high blood pressure, eat unhealthy foods and then sit
back and wonder why they are sick or their energy levels are
extremely low.

And that is exactly how life works.

We all get our mini warnings when we are
moving out of alignment spiritually, physically or emotionally.

**At that point we can either choose to pay attention or
ignore the warnings.**

If we ignore it, we soon realize that we're actually not getting
away with anything and eventually it will all catch up to us.

This speaks to the importance of discipline.

In life we will all have to do things that we don't necessarily
desire to do – however if we can do it anyway it will pay us
dividends in health, wealth and peace of mind.

**"I DISCIPLINE MYSELF SO THAT LIFE
DOESN'T HAVE TO DISCIPLINE ME"**

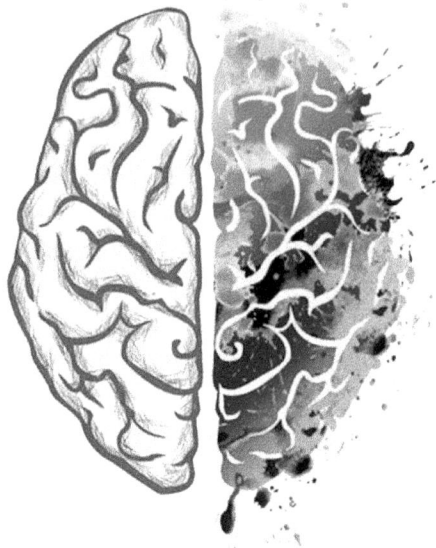

#40
DISCIPLINE

*I have learned that I really do have discipline,
self-control, and patience.
But they were given to me as a seed,
and it's up to me to choose to develop them.*

-Joyce Meyer

Discipline is not a trait that people are naturally born with.

It is generally something that is developed either by nurture from their family or by necessity from their circumstances.

Many people think of discipline as a bad word, but in actuality it is something that can help a person to thrive in every area of life.

As a free spirit myself, I have always run away from anything that seemed like it involved control or discipline.

However it wasn't until I grew older, that I fully understood the gift that comes through being specific and regimented in one's activities.

If a person follows a system or predictable methodology of doing something, they can generally rely on getting a highly predictable result.

On the other hand if a person approaches their activities with a different way of doing things each and every time, not only will they lose their efficiency – but they will be more likely to get less reliable results each time.

Discipline is a practice that can help a person in literally every area of life.

The beauty of it is - by following a consistent regimen, it slowly but surely becomes second nature.

"I AM STRONG, DISCIPLINED, AND FOCUSED, ON MY GOALS."

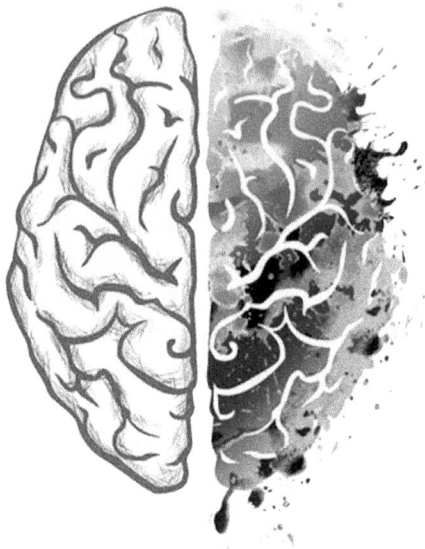

#41

FAITH

The past is a source of knowledge, and the future is a source of hope. Love of the past implies faith in the future.

-Stephen Ambrose

How do you look at your past?

Are you memories filled with anger and pain or joy and happiness?

How you talk about your childhood and your past is a very accurate indicator of how your future will look moving forward.

An example of this would be two men that have had a hard life filled with poverty and struggle.

One of them looks back on his past and talks about how he would have been successful in life, if it had not been for his rough childhood.

The other man looks back on his past and says BECAUSE of his rough childhood and the lessons he learned he became successful in life.

In order to re-frame your past, you don't have to love everything that happened to you, but you do need to release your victimization story and find your lessons from the challenges which you have experienced and figure out how you can use those lessons to help other people.

If you can go through that process, you will find yourself moving through life in a position of power – wiser and stronger as a result of the growth and lessons that you have learned along with the way.

"ALL OF MY EXPERIENCES HAVE MADE ME STRONGER AND WISER"

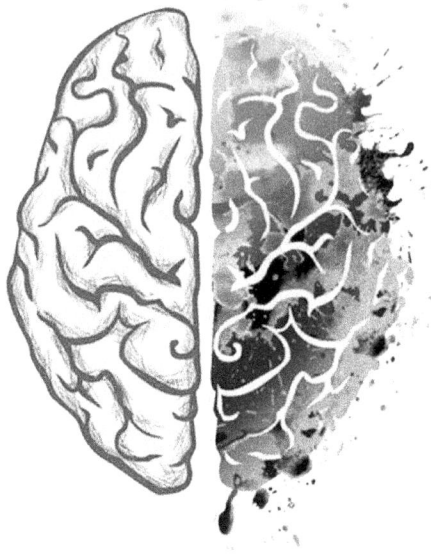

#42
FAITH

Faith is taking the first step even when you don't see the whole staircase.

-Martin Luther King, Jr.

No true growth can take place without the energy of faith in your life.

You need faith to move forward in any new activity or enterprise which you engage in because you are doing something that you have never done before.

When something is new to your subconscious mind – it doesn't know what to expect so it falls into its default job description – which is to keep you safe and comfortable.
(i.e. stay with things that are already familiar to you).

If you are going to move forward in life and grow – you are going to have to resist the temptation to stay the same, which is going to require you to have faith in the unknown.

Recognize that as you take steps forward and keep on going – that you will eventually figure it out and successfully arrive at your destination.

"I HAVE FAITH THAT I WILL SUCCESSFULLY ACHIEVE MY GOALS IF I JUST KEEP GOING"

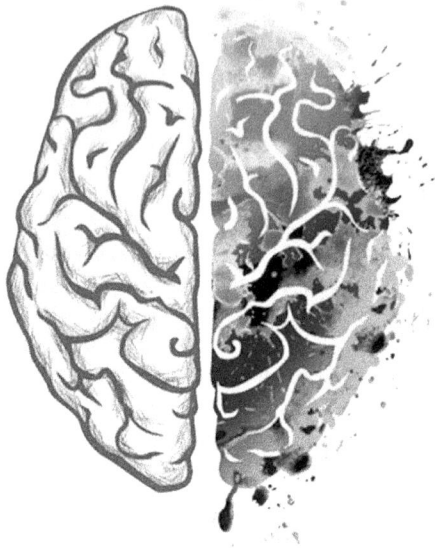

#43
FAITH

Therefore I tell you, do not worry about your life, what you will eat or drink; or about your body, what you will wear. Is not life more than food, and the body more than clothes? Look at the birds of the air: They do not sow or reap or gather into barns —and yet your Heavenly Father feeds them. Are you not much more valuable than they? Who of you worrying can add a single hour to his lifespan?

-Matthew 6:25-27
The Holy Bible

I am constantly amazed about how much people worry about things that are 100% outside of their control.

It's an interesting phenomenon actually.

In my lifetime I have been told by people on several occasions that I didn't care about certain challenges because I wasn't pacing the floor, talking about it constantly or losing sleep over it.

I believe that I have always held a subconscious belief in my spirit, that things will work out how they are supposed to work out, and me worrying, stressing and making myself sick is not going to change the outcome.

I have been shaken by the realization that for some people, the act of projecting 100,000 ways that things could go wrong is some people's sincere and conscious way of showing that they care about a situation.

However my assertion to that is these people do more harm than good.

Not only are they causing undue stress to their physical and emotional body, they are accomplishing absolutely nothing.

In the end, if you can do something to improve a situation – then do it. If you can't do anything to improve a situation, then release the emotional need to control and trust that just like the birds of the air – you will be taken care of.

"I AM ALWAYS SAFE, CARED FOR AND DIVINELY PROTECTED"

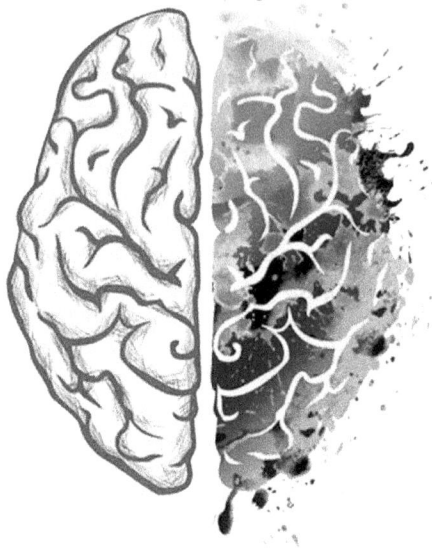

#44

FAITH

God has already done everything He's going to do.
The ball is now in your court.

If you want success, if you want wisdom, if you want to be
prosperous and healthy, you're going to have to do more
than meditate and believe; you must boldly declare
words of faith and victory over yourself and your family.

-Joel Osteen

One of the most powerful ways to shift the energy around you and get into full on "attraction mode" where things miraculously come together and work out magnificently on your behalf - is to integrate the practice of affirmations into your daily routine.

That is a huge part of why I included them in this book.

Affirmations are a way of programming your subconscious and your conscious mind to look for the desired outcome.

I have seen more and more that a lot of traditional Christian church ministries have now integrated this practice this into their message to help empower people.

They know that prayer in and of itself is only one component of the manifestation process.

In order to create a shift in your life in the form of what many would term "answered prayer", you must "BELIEVE THAT YOU RECEIVE."

One of the easiest and most effective ways to do that is to visualize being victorious and start proclaiming words to your subconscious mind so it can be on the lookout for evidence to support your victory – because it is already there!

"I AM VICTORIOUS IN EVERY AREA OF MY LIFE"

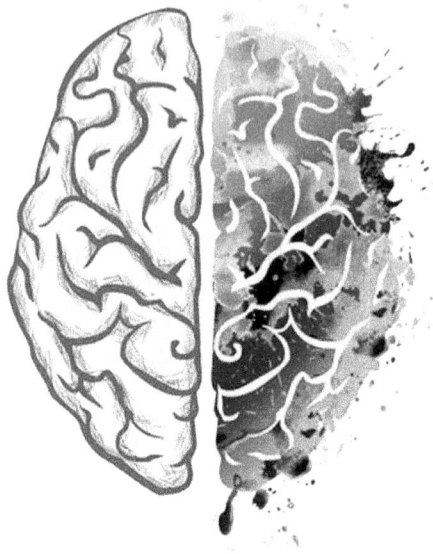

#45
WISDOM

The only true wisdom is in knowing you know nothing.

-Socrates

Have you ever met someone who was so educated
that they were kinda dumb?

Often these types of people are so busy regurgitating information,
that they don't actually use their own brain to think and analyze
information to draw their own conclusions.

Another version of this phenomenon is the person who
refuses to listen to anyone or anything because they feel
like they already know everything.

Their favorite phrase to say is "I know that" and
what happens as soon as they do, is their brain shuts down and
prevents them from hearing or learning anything else.

This kills the learning process and a person's ability to
evolve and grow.

Remember to stay open and never feel like you know anything.

There is always more to learn if you stay open and available to listen.

"I AM OPEN AND AVAILABLE TO LEARN SOMETHING NEW AT ALL TIMES"

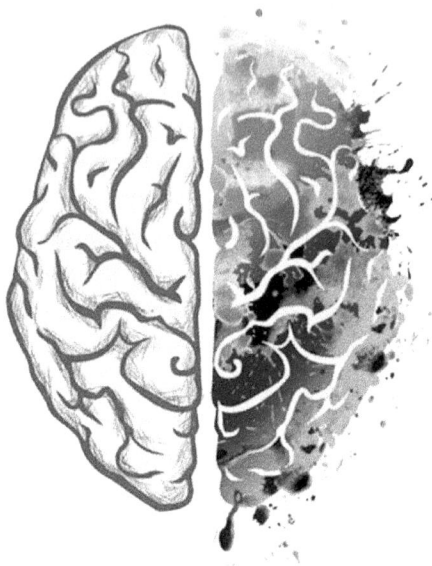

#46
WISDOM

It's not what you look at that matters, it's what you see.

-Henry David Thoreau

A few years ago I started studying Quantum Physics and I was amazed to learn about the true nature of reality as revealed by science.

Scientific studies have determined that most of the physical matter that we see in our physical space is mostly made up of open space.

This principle states that mass is really the result of focused energy and that depending on who is observing the mass and what they expect to see, the physical atoms that they are looking at will adjust.

Simply stated, our environment and the physical things that we see and experience - adjust based on both our perception of what we are seeing and our expectation of what we think we will see.

There is no such thing as reality.
There is merely YOUR REALITY.

What makes up your reality is a compilation of your experiences, your beliefs and what you have been programmed to believe from your parents, the school system, and the greater society. .

The biggest and most important challenge in our lifetime is being purposeful about what we choose to tune into and give energy to.

By doing so, we are physically creating the world around us.

"I CREATE THE WORLD I WANT TO EXPERIENCE
EVERYDAY WITH MY THOUGHTS"

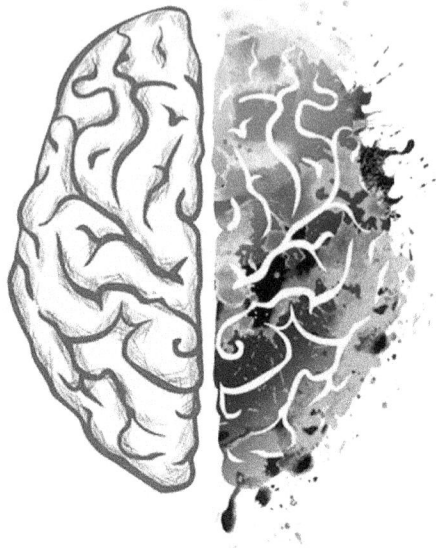

#47

WISDOM

By three methods we may learn wisdom:
First, by reflection, which is noblest;
Second, by imitation, which is easiest;
and third by experience, which is the bitterest.

-Confucius

As we evolve in wisdom and grow in maturity, we come to understand that we don't need to go through the hardships and pain that others may have already experienced – we can simply learn and choose to grow from their mistakes.

Unfortunately, many people are not willing to give up their pride, surrender their ego and just listen to the feedback and experiences of others.

Because of stubbornness, their journey is usually much more challenging and difficult than it needs to be.

When you learn to surrender – you stop fighting against life and you receive what you desire faster, because you are letting go of the resistance you have to getting what you truly want.

"I SURRENDER AND I SUBMIT TO LIFE"

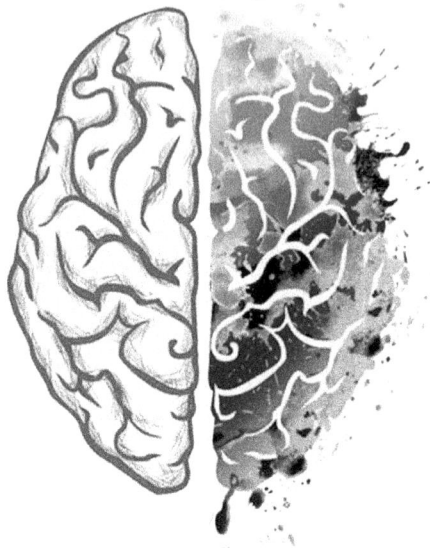

#48
WISDOM

For beautiful eyes, look for the good in others;
for beautiful lips, speak only words of kindness;
and for poise, walk with the knowledge that you are never alone.

-Audrey Hepburn

The people and situations that we attract into our life are reflections of us.

We can only see in others that which we are tuned into seeing.

If you are constantly encountering rude, angry, frustrated, broken people in your life – it is best to go home and look in the mirror to do some soul searching.

A person who is looking for the good in others and speaking words of kindness to others is automatically going to be attractive to people.

People are naturally attracted to happy people!

If you want to be admired for your beauty – learn to see the beauty in others.

"I ALWAYS LOOK FOR THE GOOD IN OTHERS"

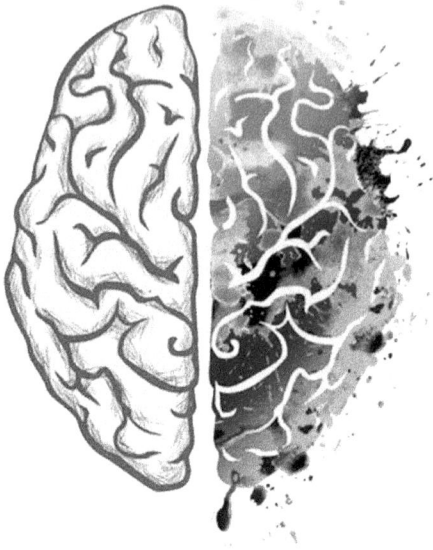

#49
ATTITUDE

People may hear your words, but they feel your attitude.

-John C. Maxwell

There is a grocery store that is not too far from my house, which I go to all of the time and there is a cashier who works their named Monica, who literally makes my day every time I see her!

She always has a smile and a cheerful word.

She is diligent and conscientious about how she bags the groceries.

Seriously – she rocks!

The last time I saw her, I literally thanked her for letting her light shine so brightly because I get a burst of energy and feel better every time I see her.

Wouldn't it be nice to have that type of affect on the people that you come into contact with everyday?

Wouldn't it be nice to have people say that they feel better and they are much happier after they leave your presence?

Well, that reality is possible if we work on having a positive attitude every day.

As we do so, that joy and happiness and love will naturally ripple out and touch others.

"I SPREAD JOY, HAPPINESS AND LOVE TO OTHERS EVERYDAY!"

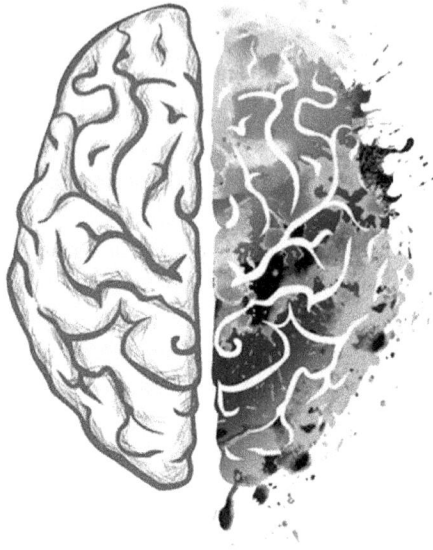

#50
ATTITUDE

If you don't like something, change it.
If you can't change it, change your attitude.

-Maya Angelou

I am always amazed at how much your average person likes to complain. I truly believe that on some level, a lot of people enjoy when something bad happens to them.

That way they can spend all day telling their "poor me" story.

They love going into detail and taking you step by step through exactly what happened, the trauma that they experienced, along with why and how they were so horribly victimized.

Those that know me well, know that this generally does not go over very well with me. I usually give people about 5 minutes maximum (if I am feeling generous) to get into their 'poor me' ritual but after that – it is totally a wrap.

I either tell them to stop, let them know I am getting off of the phone or just walk away.

Why?

Because MY mental state of mind is extremely precious and I don't have the time to allow people who are not planting anything positive to rent space in my head.

Because I understand so clearly how the law of attraction works and how we attract things into our experience based on our mindset and consciousness – I don't allow people to plant any seeds that will harvest things I do not want to experience.

Be a caretaker over your mind and don't allow other people to plant things into your subconscious that don't belong there!

"I ONLY PLANT THOUGHTS INTO MY MIND THAT I DESIRE TO HARVEST."

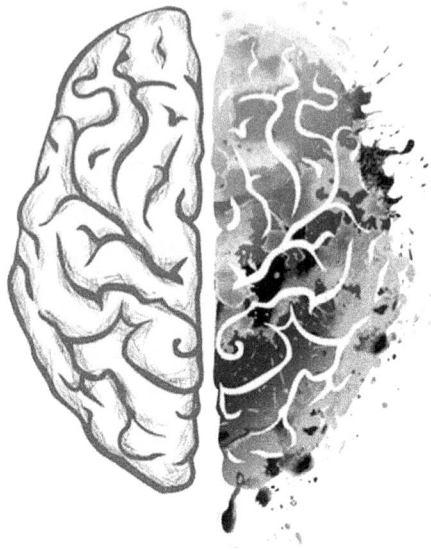

#51
ATTITUDE

Your attitude, not your aptitude, will determine your altitude.

-Zig Ziglar

Once upon a time people were taught if they were smart, got good grades and went to college and got a degree that they would get a steady well paying and secure job and have a happy, successful life.

I think most of us these days realize that story no longer applies in today's economy and that nowadays - nothing could be further from the truth.

Your success in life is not based on following the script you've been given about having to do things in a certain way in order to be successful.

For example:

Steve Jobs dropped out of college to start the Apple Corporation.

Sir Richard Branson dropped out of high school to start Virgin Records.

Mark Zuckerberg dropped out of Harvard to start Facebook.

And the list goes on and on...

So what was the common denominator of their success?

They were all **determined and focused** on accomplishing a very big goal and none of them stopped until they achieved it.

The key to massive success and achievement is not talent – it is the ability to keep going despite life's challenges.

"I AM OBSESSED WITH SUCCESS"

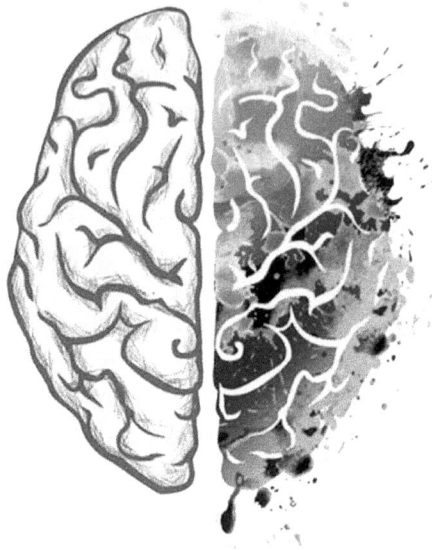

#52
ATTITUDE

The secret of genius is to carry the spirit of the child into old age, which means never losing your enthusiasm.

-Aldous Huxley

Children are unadulterated balls of wonder!

They are always excited, always curious, always motivated, and completely resilient.

You can say no to a child 999 times and they will still ask you the same question just one more time.

Be childlike in your quest for success and make sure that you approach whatever it is that you REALLY want to do for a living with the same motivation and energy as an excited two year old.

If you dwell in that space energetically, your excitement will motivate and fuel others to join your movement and buy into whatever you are doing.

"I HAVE CHILDLIKE ENTHUSIASM"

CONCLUSION

As I discussed in the beginning of this book, the subconscious mind is programmed by things that it gets exposed to repeatedly - which means that our actions are a reflection of what we have been programmed to believe.

In this book I introduced 52 mindset shifts that you can make on a daily, weekly or at will basis that will help to shift your mindset and refocus it toward the positive outcomes that you desire in your life.

Whether it is starting a new business, improving your health, or deepening your personal relationships – these 52 Ways to Reprogram Your Mind for Happiness & Success will give you the tools to make positive change in your life very quickly.

If you integrate these reprogramming sessions into your daily routine, you will undoubtedly achieve amazing results.

Visit www.jenniferdcarroll.com to get further tools, resources and training that will help you reprogram yourself for the success you desire.

ABOUT THE AUTHOR

Jennifer D. Carroll is the founder of The uFreedom Network – a lifestyle transformation organization that helps business professionals who are longing for more fulfillment and joy in their lives, surrender to their purpose so they can fall in love with their lives again!

The uFreedom Network is compromised of heart centered professionals who are devoted to using their unique skills, knowledge and talents in order to elevate the consciousness of the planet.

As a heart centered entrepreneur herself, Jennifer has a commitment to helping people obtain lifestyle freedom. She has over 12 years of experience in real estate as both a mortgage broker and real estate agent – and most recently as the owner of the credit and financial education company - Get Your Credit Perfect Now.

Jennifer has a deep devotion to the two life principles FREEDOM & SELF DETERMINATION.

She has dedicated her life to helping others to create a life of freedom for themselves and their family through financial education and entrepreneurship.

She offers lifestyle transformation coaching to help people get clear on their life's purpose, and release mental and emotional blocks that keep them from moving forward in their passion. She provides practical tools and coaching to help entrepreneurs and would be entrepreneurs get from where they are to where they want to be.

Jennifer is also a public speaker, marketing trainer, credit coach and radio/TV talk show guest who resides in Atlanta, GA.

You can learn more about Jennifer at
www.jenniferdcarroll.com

Friend her on Facebook
www.facebook.com/lifemasterywithjen

Follow her on Instagram
@jenniferdcarroll

Watch her on Youtube
www.youtube.com/jenniferdcarroll